TABLE OF CONTENTS

I0051879

First published 2016 © Errol Clive Ashwell

P. O. Box 376, Shelly Beach, KwaZulu-Natal, 4265, South Africa.

Telephone: +27 82 888 0636

Email: errol@ashwell.co.za

ISBN 978-0-620-70873-9

1. Foreword

Henning Rasmuss – Director, Paragon Group

In our businesses, I am known as the 'technology luddite'. My original 'business partner-in-crime', Anthony, will be the first one to say so. The question is: why am I writing this foreword? The answer is simple: this book is for people like me.

I am the classical 'late adopter', the kid who graduated from architecture school in 1994 into the first CAD age, but believed (honestly, I did, and so did my best friends) that computers would never draw as fast and as well as we did on our drawing boards. We were probably the last professional generation to enjoy the conviction that the skills of our hands were superior to the abilities of technology. We had no idea of what we would witness – and either grasp, or fail, to understand.

While my partner loves Technology As Such, and is a first adopter, I love What Technology Does. So that is why this book is for people like me – and you. Technology promises – but how do you make it do what it promises, for you? For your business?

I wish I had had this book (and read it) about 15 years ago. Because that is when technology first became a real differentiator – at least in architecture, our business. This book makes the process of adoption accessible. No TLA's (three-letter acronyms) and no tech-speak. No mystery and no magic. Just plain old structured reasoning and encouragement. This book talks to entrepreneurs. What do entrepreneurs need? Company. Because it's lonely out there.

Most people who read this book, will have heard about the famous Pareto Principle or the '80/20 rule'.

And how I wish I had known about this principle. You see, the problem with anyone starting a business, or starting a technology implementation, is this: you think your business, or your problem, is unique. Here's encouraging news: it's not. 80% of being in business, and remaining in business, is the same. 20% is unique. The 80% is what I share with Google. Or with Ford. Or with Kellogg's. And this book deals with what we all have in common: we actually fear technology, at the point of wanting to believe its promises.

This is the core of this book: it makes you feel good and comfortable about crossing a threshold. Reading it feels like having your hand held when you first want to jump into a swimming pool from a 3 metre diving board. Entrepreneurs are, by their nature, already outside of their comfort zone. They are where they want to be. But as I said: it gets lonely out there, and before you know it, technology is one of the Big Enemies. Instead of being the Big Enabler.

As I write this, I am looking at the diagram on page 49. How beautiful and perfect. But here's the thing: business life does not work like that. The eternal question is: 'did she jump, or was she pushed?' In business, normally, change forces change on you. And more often than not, technology adoption is reactive. Not proactive. And that is where this book helps, too. There are planned processes, but more often than not, your business will – like a child – surprise you. Just when you thought you knew what your business needed, your business will tell you what it needs. And it is not what you expected. And you feel alone. And technology promises you something. And you are back at the starting point.

So here I am, a successful architect of sorts, having worked with incredible partners and team members and clients and consultants, and we have gone down this road together, making projects and products and processes better through technology. These days, we are not adopting new CAD or BIM applications, we are adopting business process solutions to stay ahead of the competition. We optimize and measure and plan. With technology. We are just about to complete a four-year implementation of software that gives us more control over our business. And this time, we can see: the profitability and quality of life improvement the application promised, is being achieved. We set out to make our lives better, to spend more time with the people who matter to us, and to make better use of the most amazing resource we have: people. And it is working.

But we would have gotten there faster, and easier, and with more buy-in, if we had read this book four years ago.

This is really a 'how-to' book and contains much advice. Without having to add any, I will nonetheless.

- One: Treat your reseller as a partner, and not as the guy or girl who owns the company from which you make a grudge purchase. This means selecting the reseller carefully, and choosing someone you like to work with.

- Two: On the periphery of the global economy, including South Africa where we work, realize this: product support may lurk in the US or elsewhere, and there is a good chance that you have to import your own support team from somewhere on earth. And then have your reseller ask if he or she can join your training sessions in your office. It has happened to us.

Speaking as a Technology Luddite, I can only say: this book makes me want to go down the next technology route. Against my strong instincts.

Henning Rasmuss

Sandton, Gauteng, South Africa. 2016.

The Creative Counsel Head Office, Corlett Drive, Johannesburg
Designed by Anthony Orelowitz at Paragon Architects

2. Acknowledgements

To Henning Rasmuss for agreeing to and writing the foreword to this book. It is much appreciated and an honour indeed! You are one of those rare individuals who is not only passionate about his business, but also his profession, his country and society at large. Your participation in making the world a better and more beautiful place is really appreciated.

Henning's leadership is reflected in Paragon Architects and the Paragon Group achieving world-class celebrity in their field. His belief in the role of enabling technology to help skilled people to maximise their potential serves as a shining example to others. Thank you Henning.

A huge thank you to Anne Logan, Marc Ashwell and Kim Ashwell. Your support, ruthless constructive criticism and suggestions have improved this book more than you can be aware! And to Marc for the design of the cover and so many good ideas – your talent never ceases to amaze me!

To Gareth Modena, for validating the content and keeping it real. You have guided so many technology projects to successful conclusion over the years that you can spot process errors or omissions from a mile away (or even 1.60934 Km). Thank you, Gareth.

A grateful acknowledgement to Leonard Nimoy for the name of the final chapter. Nimoy, playing Mr. Spock in the original Star Trek television series, personally devised the now-famous Vulcan Salute. Thank you also to Gene Roddenberry, the creator of Star Trek, for a series that introduced fantastic new technologies to our imaginations, but always kept the technology in its place: The technology was always there to support and enable the people. Human advancement and success remained the show's raison d'etre.

Finally, thank you to the hundreds of thousands (if not millions) of unsung heroes working in the technology companies that bring us the advanced technologies that enable us mere mortals to realise giant leaps in performance and capability. It is your genius and dedication that helps move society positively forward!

Errol Ashwell

Shelly Beach, KwaZulu-Natal, South Africa. 2016.

3.   Dedication

This book is dedicated to Dalene Ashwell – my friend, partner, companion and loving wife of 43 years. For all of the support through thick and thin, ups and downs, and all the wonderful years. You have kept me moving forward and the reason that this book is finally complete. You are the love of my life!

4.   Introduction

Enabling Technology

So what is 'enabling technology'? Google will offer you dozens of answers. I believe that BusinessDictionary.com explains it best: Enabling Technology is *"Equipment and/or methodology that alone or in combination with associated technologies, provides the means to generate giant leaps in performance and capability"*.

In other words, this is technology that *helps people to do and achieve more* – not replace their knowledge and skills. The phrase of real interest to the business person is naturally *"… giant leaps in performance and capability"*. That is quite a promise! And it is such promises that I believe this book will be able to help you to realise in *your* business environment – leading, when ultimately successful, to competitive advantage.

Still not sure what can be considered 'enabling technology'? Let's take a look at some examples of technologies so momentous that, with their invention and adoption, enabled *"giant leaps in performance and capability"* – thus dramatically changing the world in which we live.

The Industrial Revolution – Leading to the Industrial Age

The years 1760 to 1870 saw the introduction of so many enabling technologies that we now refer to that time as the Industrial Revolution. A revolution indeed. Up to that time, production was typically achieved directly by human or animal effort – placing very distinct limits on how much could be achieved in any given time.

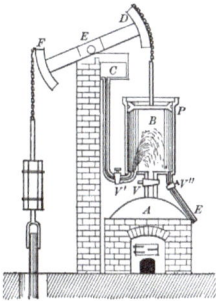

The first and possibly most significant *"giant leap"* came with the invention of the steam engine and its widespread adoption as a replacement for water power or animal power in industry and transportation. This became the era of the machine: The invention of machine tools, such as lathes and milling machines used to cut metal quickly and accurately, began to be used to make the parts for even more complex machines.

Advances in the development of materials was rapid. Iron, steel, cement and concrete-making technology also improved dramatically, enabling the construction of huge building and infrastructure projects – and even better machines.   The textile and transportation industries were examples of industries that literally changed the world – and early adopters of the necessary enabling technologies in those industries became the first industrialist millionaires and billionaires. The 'Industrial Age' had arrived.

The Computer Revolution

Whilst analogue computing machines had been invented and developed since the 19th century – and were famously used during the 2nd World War both for weapons guidance and cryptography amongst other things – it is the invention and rapid development of the 'Electronic Digital Computer', that really changed the world into that in which we live today.

The honour of inventing the first electronic digital computer goes to John Vincent Atanasoff (1903 – 1995), an American physicist and inventor, who built it during the late 1930s at Iowa State College together with his student, Clifford Berry. Sadly, although perhaps I should say inevitably, commercial interests led to this honour being challenged. However, in 1973 the challenges were resolved when the judge in the Honeywell vs. Sperry Rand lawsuit ruled that Atanasoff was the indeed the inventor of the electronic digital computer.

John Atanasoff – Father of the Digital Computer

The invention of the electronic digital computer was to our world today what the invention of the steam engine was to the world 150 years before. The computer became the device that provided the "*means to generate giant leaps in performance and capability*" in almost every line of human endeavour. The invention, during the late 1940s, of the transistor and then the integrated-circuit (microchip), led to the gradual miniaturisation of digital computers, so that today we find them able to be used inside the tiniest of devices.

The 1960s saw the introduction of computerisation on a huge scale, unprecedented access to information and the rise of the knowledge economy. The 'Information Age' had arrived.

Enabling Technology in the Information Age

Most of us in business today entered the business world during the 'Information Age' – and most of the enabling technology inventions have themselves been enabled by the rapid advances in computer technology. I have spent my entire career (more than forty years) helping companies to improve their businesses by underpinning and/or automating business processes with the effective implementation of enabling technologies.

I have been involved with many enabling technologies during my career – all of which have provided the *"means to generate giant leaps in performance and capability"* and all of which I have seen successfully adopted by companies, enabling them to enjoy significant competitive advantage:

In the Electronics Industry

- The invention and adoption of 'Automated Test Equipment' (ATE) technology that enabled computer-automated testing and fault diagnosis of electronic components and electronic assemblies – without the need for technicians to undertake manual tests with banks of measuring and diagnostic equipment.

In the Printing Industry

- The adoption of new computerised 'Phototypesetting' technology as a replacement for hand-set type or the use of 'hot metal' typesetting machines.

Linotype composing room of the Chicago Defender newspaper

- The arrival of computer systems for the manipulation, retouching and colour-correction of scanned photographs and images in preparation for printing. The adoption of this enabling technology eliminated the need for complicated and time-consuming photographic techniques using black and white colour-separations, retouched by hand. This technology has continued to develop and move into our everyday world: Who is not familiar with Adobe's 'Photoshop®' today?

- The development and adoption of computerised 'Full Page Make Up' technology that enabled entire pages to be designed and composed on a computer screen and output ready for printing, as opposed to the necessity of numerous photographic processes and manual composition of dozens of film, type and line elements by highly-skilled craftsmen.

In the Business World

- The arrival and adoption of computerised 'Word Processing' technology – replacing the typewriter and 'Tipp-Ex®' – which increased office productivity by an inestimable amount.

- The invention and adoption of the 'Spreadsheet' computer application that revolutionised the speed and accuracy of producing business forecasts and reports, and opened the door to the practical implementation of 'what-if' scenario calculations in our everyday business lives.

- Adoption of 'Customer Relationship Management' (CRM) technology in the world of sales. Such CRM systems contain every detail about your products and customers – and every detail of every sales or service interaction. They also often integrate with your accounting system to include the automation of processes such as quoting and invoicing. CRM systems provide sales managers with sales reports and statistics. The nett business benefit is the enabling of effective sales management and giant leaps in sales productivity.

- The more recent invention and adoption of 'Marketing Automation' applications – used to automate numerous marketing and communication activities between the company and its prospective customers. Intelligently analysing who is looking at what in your emails or on your website, this technology is the enabler behind the fast-growing trend of 'inbound marketing' and online purchasing that is revolutionising the world of sales and commerce.

In the Design and Engineering Industry

- The arrival of 'Computer-Aided Drafting' (CAD) software aimed at replacing the drawing board and pencil that had been the standard tools of the draughtsman's trade for centuries. Closely following computer-aided drafting, came 'Computer-Aided Design' technology (still using the 'CAD' or 'CADD' acronym) that was subtly more sophisticated in that it offered an ever-growing range of tools to assist in *design* processes in addition to the *drawing* process.

- The development and adoption of computerised three-dimensional (3D) modelling applications for designers, architects and engineers that have revolutionised the entire field of design and engineering. Such 'Model-Based Design' applications enable easy-to-understand 3D visualisations of a product, building or engineering project. Traditional 2D drawings are simply a by-product extracted from the model – if required at all.

Courtesy Adept Airmotive
South Africa

- The addition of 'intelligence' to computer design and engineering models, incorporating all component specifications such as material, strength, vendor, weight, finish, quantities etc. These attributes and sophisticated algorithms enable the function and performance of these models to be simulated, analysed and tested prior to physical prototypes being made or actual construction being started.

These examples are not an exhaustive list by any means. However, they are all examples of enabling technologies that have had the power to unlock competitive advantage for successful adopters. Thinking perhaps that the sales pitch often sounds too good to be true? Forty years of experience in this field has also proven that there has been little change to the process of successfully ensuring that the promise of business benefits are actually realised. Realising 'the promise' is what this book is about.

It is important to point out that enabling technologies do not replace or displace skilled people. In most cases in our businesses, we still depend on human skills, expertise and experience. Enabling technologies are all about enabling skilled *people* to do more and achieve more. Enabling our businesses to realise a competitive advantage.

Please do not be confused: This is *very* different from – if not the opposite of – 'automation technology' that is designed to *replace* the human element. Automation is typically designed to replace repetitive manual tasks and execute them faster and more accurately – eventually removing people from the equation altogether.

Ubiquitous Technology

You will have realised from the above that as time moves on, an 'enabling technology' – even a very dramatic one – eventually becomes commonplace. It gets to a point that the technology becomes so ubiquitous, that its use is pretty much mandatory and will not really contribute any longer to competitive advantage. Of course there are always examples of laggard adopters who place themselves at competitive *dis*advantage by waiting too long and allowing their competitors to 'eat their lunch'! Their chances of remaining in business are usually slim.

So, in this book I have specifically excluded from my definition of 'enabling technology', all technologies that are so fundamental and inescapable today, that there is no decision involved as to whether or not they should be adopted in our businesses. We are seriously unlikely to be plagued with decisions such as "Should we use the wheel?", "Should we use digital computers?", "Should we use electricity?" or "Should we use telephones?" These technologies are so pervasive today that you do not need to read a book about how to make them work for your business!

'The Internet' is an interesting technology, in that it can be debated as to whether or not it is an 'enabling technology' in the sense used in this book. My rationalisation is that the Internet is now so fundamental and pervasive that we really have no option but to embrace it as a business tool. Therefore it is no longer an 'enabling technology' in and of itself. However, its incredible impact on society and business – and its usage as a platform for many other enabling technologies – is so revolutionary that it demands further exploration in the following chapter.

5.   The Connected Age

Farewell to the Information Age

As said before, most of us in business today entered the business world during the 'Information Age'. Many people believe we are still in the Information Age – and many businesses act as if they are still in the Information Age. But the reality is that connectivity and the 'Internet of Things' is changing everything.

Today, everyone and everything is interconnected.   We are now squarely in the 'Connected Age'. Social behaviour and relationships have changed forever. Business models   and   economies   have changed forever.   Learning and education have changed forever. Opportunities for collaboration have exploded. While Microsoft had exemplified the 'Information Age', Google and Apple now exemplify the dawn of the 'Connected Age'.

And Business Will Never Be the Same Again…

Just twenty years ago, the world of business was a *very* different place. Business was orderly. Business obeyed the classic rules of marketing and sales.

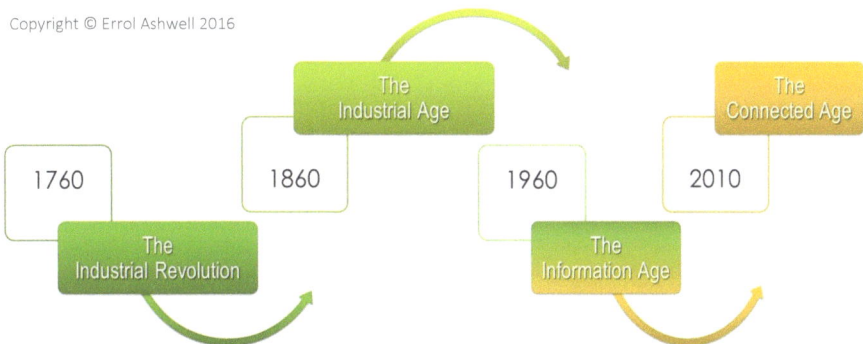

Stores on Main Street or in shopping malls sold books and CDs. People waited patiently in line for a teller at the bank. People browsed in their favourite shop for the latest hobby supplies and books, model cars, trains or planes. Collectors combed through auctions, car boot sales and antique shops. You booked your travel through a travel agent and rented DVD movies at a video rental store. Cinemas showed movies projected from real 35mm film!

Business was a predictable, logical world. The five-year plan mapped out your future. There was a comfortable sense of commercial security and business longevity.

Then the whole world changed – never to be the same again. The Connected Age had arrived...

If you own, manage or operate a business that is more than ten years old, that business has either changed dramatically or is in urgent in need of a major overhaul. A business that is less than ten years old has either embraced this new world – or is about to go out of business.

The author dwarfed by a 35mm cinema projector from his collection

The Connected World is Different

The real problem is that many people in business do not realise that the world *has* actually changed! Or they do not appreciate the extent of that complete and dramatic change. Change that means that everything they learned about building a business; about competitive strategy; about communication; about marketing; about sales; about product delivery; about customer service; no longer holds true. The business world is irreversibly *different*!

First the Internet, then email, then the World Wide Web, then web search (particularly Google), then social media, tablet computers, smartphones and other mobile devices, then 'The Cloud' and the 'Internet of Things' ... then ... and then?

The world of business has been taken by surprise – not only the increasingly rapid rate of these developments – but the effect that this technology has had on the *way business is done*.

Do people still have needs? Of course they do. Do people still buy? Of course they do. Do they still buy for the same reasons? Yes they do. Do we still need to tell them about our products and services? Sure. So what has changed so dramatically? Connectivity has *enabled* buyers to buy the way they have always wanted to: People do not *want* to queue at the bank. They do not *want* to rely on salespeople to provide them with information about new products. They do not *want* to be restricted to the choice of merchandise that the local store just happens to have in stock.

For most businesses still living in the 'Information Age', the biggest surprise comes from the unprecedented rate at which these technologies and social changes are being embraced and adopted by the world at large. The 'Connected Age' has not only changed the way business is done, it has *rapidly* changed – and is still changing – the way people live, think, learn, work and play.

So what does any of this have to do with enabling competitive advantage? In a word: Everything!

The companies that are now forming, growing and becoming incredibly successful in the Connected Age are those led by visionaries who understand people's frustrations, understand what customers really want (or would want if it existed) and who have been brave enough to envisage, develop and deliver something completely new and different.

Jeff Bezos
Founder and CEO Amazon.com

The business success stories of the young 'Connected Age' are stories of competitive advantage won through innovation, by people who embrace change. The business success stories of the near future will be of visionary leaders who have realised *"giant leaps in performance and capability"* by embracing further connectivity and adopting enabling technologies that are possibly only now being invented.

Enabling Technology in the Connected Age

Technologies being developed in the 'Connected Age', are promising business benefits to be realised from dramatically improved connectivity: Improved business processes; sharing of information; improved collaboration; improved human productivity and effectiveness; improved business information; significantly improved decision making capabilities and improved profitability.

As an example of enabling technology in the 'Connected Age', let's take a look at developments in the world of design and engineering. Whilst this may not be a field familiar to you, I am sure that everyone can appreciate that the design and development of any new product, facility, or infrastructure project is a major undertaking indeed.

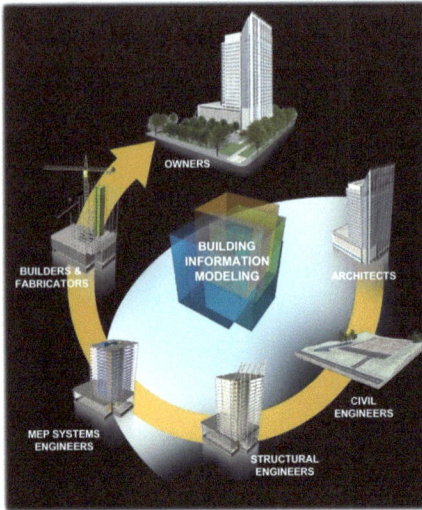

Although a dream born in the 'Information Age', there has long been a desire to see the management of such projects fully integrated end-to-end using information technology from initial concept through design to construction or manufacture, then everyday use, management, maintenance and eventual demolition or scrapping.

This concept is known as 'Building Information Modelling' (BIM) in the case of buildings, process plants, mines, utilities and infrastructure, and 'Product Lifecycle Management' (PLM) in the case of manufactured products. Both BIM and PLM are based on a digital representation of physical and functional characteristics of a facility or product, creating a shared knowledge resource and forming a reliable basis for coordination, collaboration and decision making throughout that item's lifecycle, from conception to end of life.

BIM is not 'CAD' or a software application (or even range of applications), but rather a methodology and processes – underpinned by appropriate technology. BIM is an information-based interoperable modelling paradigm that sets standards for typical processes and computer-based exchanges of information amongst all stakeholders involved in the project, including designers, engineers, builders and manufacturers, construction crews, owners, asset managers, maintenance teams and commercial operators.

With enabling technologies to underpin these processes, The 'Connected Age' is enabling the BIM/PLM methodology dream to become a reality. High-speed digital communication, collaboration and project management are now possible, regardless of where in the world stakeholders may be situated.

6.   Truths About Enabling Technology

Does Enabling Technology Really Work?

I talk to a lot of people about enabling technology. Two very common reactions are "XYZ technology does not work" and "We did not get a return on our investment in XYZ" – or similar. Let's address these themes…

The (very common) question "Does this technology really work?" reminds me of the question "Does this camera take good photos?" (to which the best answer is "Yes, just like this pencil does good sketches"). It requires a person to take good photographs and a person to create a good sketch. The tool must be adequate – preferably good – but the tool alone does not do the job. A great photographer can produce great photographs with a mediocre camera. But a poor photographer with an excellent camera will most likely produce only poor results.

In the same way, the enabling technology must be adequate for the purpose – preferably good – but the technology alone does not determine whether or not it will 'work'. Even with the very best technology solution, if it is not customised to suit your business processes, if the organisation leadership does not get behind it and – most importantly – if people do not use it, then it will, by definition, be a failure. Conversely if well customised, well supported by the leaders and adopted by all, an enabling technology will certainly 'work'.

What is Success?

This book is about realising the promise of enabling technology. So success in this context must be defined as the realisation of the outcomes that you believed you would enjoy when you decided to invest in the technology in the first place. At its highest degree, realising that promise should enable you to enjoy tangible competitive advantage.

Will Enabling Technology Generate an ROI?

A 'successful' implementation of enabling technology will, by definition, generate a return on investment (ROI). However, quantifying the ROI is the tricky bit! It all depends on how you measure the ROI.

You may not be able to build a business case or measure the ROI in simple monetary terms! Unlike owning gold or property or other tangible assets, there is no intrinsic value in the ownership of most enabling technologies. It is only in the adoption and effective use of such technologies that an organisation can realise a financial benefit.

Therefore, the only meaningful way to measure the return generated by the investment in enabling technology is to measure the improvements realised with the technology in use vs. the situation prior to its implementation. If quarterly revenues increased by (say) 20% with the technology in use, then chances are you would be very happy with such a return on investment!

"But – But – But…" I Hear You Say

"But how can you attribute an increase in revenues (or productivity or profitability or whatever) to the particular technology?" A good question – enabling technology will certainly not generate revenue by itself. The answer comes back to people: If the technology enables marketers to produce more and better opportunities; enables salespeople to be more effective and more productive; or enables designers to produce better designs in less time; then surely it is reasonable to give the technology some credit for the improvements?

The secret to measuring the ROI on enabling technology implementations is to determine a realistic benchmark of 'before and after' measurable business outcomes. What do you believe is the 'promise' of the technology in question? What 'giant leaps' will you realise? In other words, a formal Business Case against which ultimate success and ROI can be measured.

When is the Best Time to Implement?

Do we jump in at the 'bleeding edge' of a new technology or do we wait until it has 'completely proven itself'? Canvass a cross-section of the people in your company and you will probably find opinions at both extremes and a range in between too! The same is true of organisations as a whole: There will always be Early Adopters, Mainstream Adopters and Laggards. This is the nature of people and of businesses.

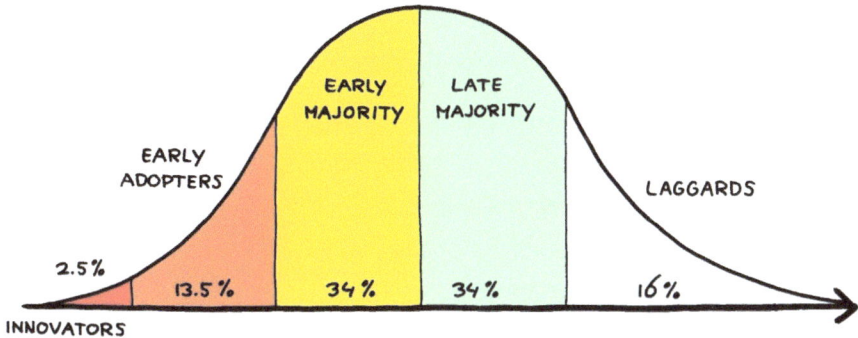

Early adopters may pay more and certainly run the risk of getting burned. However, in my experience, if early adopters follow the rules and ensure the success of the technology implementation, they are the most likely to enjoy significant competitive advantage and win.

The early majority enjoy less risk of failure and probably have to invest less overall, but will enjoy less competitive advantage. However, for the late majority there is not likely any competitive advantage in adopting what has become 'normal', 'required' or 'standard practice' in an industry.

And what of the laggards? Just as they are slow to adopt, they are also usually slow to succeed. In a high-tech world, technology laggards are usually on the road to a slow death.

Are You Prepared to Work for Success?

Ensuring adoption of a new enabling technology – and thereby guaranteeing its success – is not easy. There will *always* be significant resistance and opposition to the change! That resistance can come from any or every level of person in your company or from any department. There will always be people who are unwilling or too lazy to change. There may even be aggressive opposition from those who may have a vested interest in the status quo.

Ensuring adoption of a new technology takes time, investment and effort. It takes significant planning, change management and *leadership*. It requires a carefully balanced – and ongoing – mix of People, Processes *and* Technology.

So Why Should We Bother?

The reason we go to all this trouble and expense is obviously so that we can enjoy the business benefits and rewards that will accrue from a successful implementation. The outcomes include both promoting the positive and preventing the negative. For example:

- We establish a competitive advantage in our market.
- We differentiate ourselves from our competitors.
- We improve our reputation.
- We improve customer response times.
- We increase our revenues.
- We increase our proficiency and productivity.
- We increase our quality.
- We increase innovation.
- We decrease our costs.
- We increase our profitability.
- We reduce our time to market.
- We add additional capabilities and capacity.
- We catch up to our competitors.
- We get to remain in business.

7.   The Recipe for Success

Success or Failure is a Choice

The horror stories about failed technology implementations – and especially computer or information technology implementations – are legion:

- "What a waste of time and money that was. We never saw any return on our investment."

- "We tried to use it. But we eventually gave up. It's just a very expensive white elephant."

- "Of course we tried to use it. But the system does not work. What a waste of money!"

We've all heard these stories. You may even be one of those recounting your own horror story. But, of course, the successes inevitably outweigh the failures by a large margin. If they did not, the incredible spread and use of technology over the past few decades would simply not have happened.

But why do some technology implementations succeed while others fail miserably? I have spent my entire career helping companies to improve their businesses by underpinning or automating business processes with enabling technology. During this time it has become crystal clear why some implementations fail, while others succeed. And the answer is not luck or chance! Success can be guaranteed, as can a return on investment. In the chapters that follow, I will show you how to realise the promise of enabling technology *if you so choose.*

Disclaimer

Please notice that I am restricting my expertise and experience claim to 'enabling technology' and also keeping it in the context of driving business success.   (For any one person to claim to be able to advise on the use of *any* technology in *any* context would, of course, be ridiculous and he/she would probably also be being less than truthful!)

Ensuring Success

We all want success – and sometimes we achieve success. Other times, we may fail. Why is that? In the case of implementing enabling technologies, it generally boils down to making choices and following a tried and tested process: Following the process can almost guarantee success, whilst ignoring the process inevitably leads to failure.

You want a dinner party to be a success? Choosing a menu that will appeal to all the guests is a great start in the choices department. If you are a skilled cook, then deciding to cook the meal yourself is another step towards success. Now carefully following proven recipes to prepare all the dishes, virtually guarantees your success. All that remains is for you to enjoy being the charming host.

In this simple example, what was needed for success was making the right decisions and doing the right things at the right time by following a proven recipe. Simple, right? Well, yes it is!

The return on an investment in enabling technology will only be realised if and when the expected business outcomes are realised. So, the answer to ensuring success lies in following a proven process to make the right decisions and effectively implement the technology – leading ultimately to the realisation of the business outcomes.

Recognising Success When it Arrives

When designing and implementing an enabling technology, the focus should not be on system functionality, but on the business, people and process changes that you expect to implement – i.e. the behaviours you need to instil and the outcomes you expect to receive. Successful outcomes will only come in the wake of successful change.

When you see the changes in behaviour happening and the outcomes being realised, then you will have a successful implementation that 'works'! However, there is a major caveat: Only when there is widespread adoption of the technology – i.e. all relevant team members are using it as intended – can the implementation be deemed 'successful'.

Does Outcome Success = Competitive Advantage?

A good question! In other words, does the 'successful adoption' of an enabling technology automatically translate into competitive advantage? The answer is only 'yes' if the adoption of that technology drives a business benefit and not simply a technical benefit.

Competitive advantage stems from being able to offer something better than your competitors – improvements in response time; quality; innovation; price; reliability; service and support; or whatever. If the enabling technology helps you to achieve such business improvements, then this should be translatable directly into competitive advantage.

But What if My Competitors all do the Same?

The sad reality is that many well-intended technology implementations are not successful. This means that many organisations invest the money and a lot of time without reaping the promised rewards. Why? Well that will hopefully become clear as you read on.

When you succeed with your implementation – and you will if you follow this recipe for success – you will have realised the promise of enabling technology. And because that is relatively rare, you will also have enabled your organisation to enjoy a significant competitive advantage not easily duplicated by your competitors!

8. Active Leadership

Before we get into the process proper, let's pause to talk about leadership:

Realising the technology promise is all (and pretty much only) about leadership. Let's be *very* clear about this: Simply approving the capex investment for a new technology and/or issuing an edict that such technology shall be used from now on, will *not* ensure success. It may not even get the process moving!

The successful implementation and adoption of an enabling technology requires what I call 'Active Leadership'. This means that the leadership hierarchy must not only approve it, they must become – and *be seen to become* – an active part of the implementation and adoption process. If relevant managers and leaders are perceived to not care about the results of the project then it is inevitably doomed to irrelevance and failure.

The Story of The Race

Let's use an imaginary story as a metaphor for your technology implementation: You happen to have a few hundred million burning a hole in your pocket and you decide that it would be cool to get into, and become a contender in, the Formula One racing game.

You do some research and then go out and buy the latest and best Formula One car that you can find. There is this young man in your company that is into racing and you appoint him as the designated driver. He is very excited at the opportunity and is very happy as you send him off to the car manufacturer's facility where he is trained how to drive this magnificent machine.

Upon his return, he practises for a few weeks at a local track and is then packed off to his first Formula One event. What are his chances of winning? Of course, absolutely zero. What are his chances of at least getting a place? Still zero.

So what have we learned from this story so far? Simply investing in the technology means nothing. Even investing in the very best technology and excellent training in the use of that technology, means nothing. The technology and end-user training are only the first steps towards winning.

What our designated driver needs to learn, of course, is not only how to drive the car – but how to become a contender in a Formula One race! He needs to understand and practise the processes and techniques necessary to win. He needs a pit crew and a management crew, a race strategy and tactics to win. He needs coaching and mentoring by those who have done this before.

The whole team needs to be focused on one thing and one thing only – winning the race. And the whole team needs to see *your* involvement, *your* enthusiasm and *your* presence at practice and on the day. Achieving success needs to become all-consuming.

Can your team eventually claim that win? Of course they will!

Active Leadership

What this metaphor demonstrates is the need for a careful and continuous balancing of People, Processes *and* Technology. All three are needed and all three in balance. This is the role of leadership – and it is required continuously. The leader must be – and be seen to be – actively and meaningfully involved at all times. This is Active Leadership.

9.   The Implementation Process

Here we start to examine and unpack the proven process for realising the promise of enabling technology. But where to start?

The king in 'Alice's Adventures in Wonderland' had some great advice: "Begin at the beginning," the King said, very gravely, "and go on till you come to the end: then stop."

This quotation accurately describes the logic and simplicity of the process to successfully implement a new enabling technology.

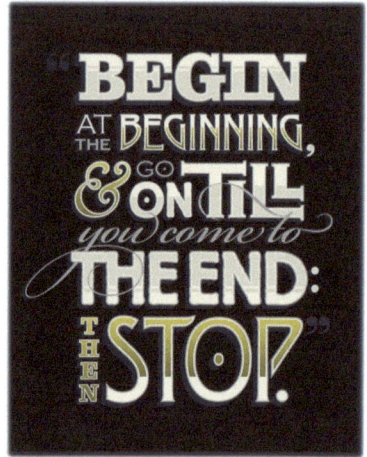

1. Begin at the Beginning...

Ask yourself: 'What problem are we trying to solve?' It is impossible to overemphasise how critical this initial step actually is. Failure to answer this question (or failure to answer it correctly) is the first step towards failure.

You have all heard the old warning that you cannot automate a process that does not work manually. This is even worse: Attempting to implement a technology that is not suited to solving your problem will achieve nothing, except wasting your team's time and putting a large dent your bank balance.

You should spend a long time – what may even seem to be a disproportionate amount of time – considering these questions: What are we trying to solve? Are we trying to increase sales? Are we trying to cut costs? Are we trying to increase productivity? Are we trying to increase profitability? Are we trying to increase capacity? Are we trying to add a new capability? Or what?

Why are we not succeeding in achieving these objectives now? What is stopping us from implementing new procedures and developing our people to achieve this right now, without any new technology? Only when you are sure that you know what you are trying to solve and why – *and* what solution is required – *and* that an appropriate enabling technology will help – should you move on.

Involve your colleagues in seeking these answers. Run internal brainstorming sessions. Employ an outside consultant to conduct interviews and facilitate focus groups or workshops. *It is that important.* It is the foundation for everything that you are about to do and achieve.

2. Undertake a Business Process Analysis

Except for a major problem or an implementation project in a large organisation, I am not about to suggest that a full professional Business Process Analysis is always required. However, in most cases, it is necessary to at least undertake a formal assessment of your current business processes, analyse and highlight opportunities for improvement, and then consider how these processes could possibly be improved with appropriate enabling technology.

This could be done internally or with the assistance of the consultant used during the interviews and workshops as described above. A thorough analysis will show what is working, what is not and what you expect to be solved/improved by the new technology.

When working with clients, I typically ensure that the formal business process analysis at least covers the following:

- **The Problem Statement**: This is the formal answer to the 'What problem are we trying to solve?' question as discussed above.

- **The Project Scope**: A statement of what is to be included in and what is to be excluded from the project on which we are about to embark. In other words, keeping it real and manageable.

- **The Desired Outcome**: The project goal formulated as a formal statement of what would we like to see as the ideal outcome(s). It is very likely that different people in the organisation will have different views about this – and that is okay at the start. Individual interviews should capture the views of the various stakeholders that should then be collated and prioritised according to role. The opinions of the organisation leadership and the project sponsor obviously carry the most weight.

- **The Project Sponsor**: Appointing the person who is the ultimate authority with respect to the project. The person who determines if things are okay or not and who eventually signs off the implementation as complete. This is *not a nominal role*. It is an 'Active Leadership' role demanding continuous engagement if the implementation is to succeed.

- **The Process Flow and Activity Descriptions**: This is the bulk of the work and lists the steps completed by relevant stakeholders in their roles. This is also where current problems are highlighted and where wish-list elements can be specified.

- **The Business Rules**: A formal statement of the business rules to which the desired solution must adhere.

- **Exceptions**: A listing of allowable alternative process paths designed to cater for exceptions to the norm.

- **Process Inputs and Criteria**: Determination of what inputs are required to start the process and the allowable formats of such inputs.

- **Process Outputs and Criteria**: Determination of what outputs are expected from the process and the allowable formats of such outputs.

- **Workflow Diagram**: A visual representation of the process showing the primary activities and the exceptions. Such a diagram is very useful for communication the process at a glance – especially to those not already intimately involved.

3. Develop the Business Case

This is a formal summary of the business benefits to be realised from the successful outcome of the project. This is the critical element that defines the benchmark against which we will ultimately (over time) measure the ROI and determine whether the project has succeeded – or failed.

4. Choose the Technology

Rest assured that when someone tells you their implementation horror story and claims that "the technology did not work", what they really mean is that they chose the wrong technology for the problem at hand or they did not implement it correctly. In this day and age, it is highly unlikely to find technology offerings that simply do not work – especially if sticking to reputable brand names.

If it makes business sense, do *not* be afraid of 'following the herd'. There used to be a saying that "Nobody got fired for buying IBM". At the time, that was pretty much true. IBM had a reputation for reliability. Their products may not have had every bell and whistle – but they worked.

When choosing in which technology solution to invest; reputation, reliability, after-sales support, ease of use and suitability for purpose are far more important considerations than fancy features. Will it solve your business problem? Have other people invested successfully in this technology? Are other people happy with the service and support from this vendor?

If you are part of a larger enterprise, beware of the fallacy that large enterprises need bespoke solutions as their needs are somehow unique. In my experience truly unique requirements are few and far between!

Needless to say, ensuring that they technology solution will solve your 'Problem Statement' as determined above, trumps all other considerations. If you are still left with a choice of vendors – follow the herd. There is probably a very good reason why one particular vendor has more customers than others!

One caveat though with respect to computer hardware: Beware of assuming that all computer hardware is similar, and that if the specifications are similar then it does not matter if IT or Procurement simply order computers from their favourite vendor. This is a fallacy – and can be a serious mistake.

Many enabling technology applications – especially those that are highly 3D graphics, engineering or scientific calculation intensive – require the computer hardware to be specifically optimised to run those applications efficiently and effectively – otherwise end-user productivity will suffer dramatically. Work with your chosen Implementation Partner (as discussed immediately below) to help you make this important decision.

5. Choose the Implementation Partner

Many Years of Experience Rule 1: *Never* make the final technology decision before finding a suitable implementation partner. When about to implement a complex technology solution – especially in the high technology realm – consider very carefully who is going to help you to implement it. At the risk of sounding over-dramatic, this is a success or failure decision.

It may seem relatively simple to decide on a big-name technology: For example SAP, Oracle or Microsoft for major enterprise applications; Salesforce.com for CRM; Microsoft for office applications; Autodesk for design and engineering applications; or whatever. That is the easy bit.

But all you end up with is 'n' licences to use a particular software technology. Those software developers are *not* going to install, configure, customise, train, implement and inspire adoption for you. They are not going to be at your side to ensure that you enjoy great success. The software alone is not the solution to your business problem.

Many Years of Experience Rule 2: *Never* try to implement it yourself. Chances are good that implementing technology solutions is not your forte as a business. Yes, you might have an IT department. But implementing complex business solutions is probably not their forte either. This is the route to the dark side.

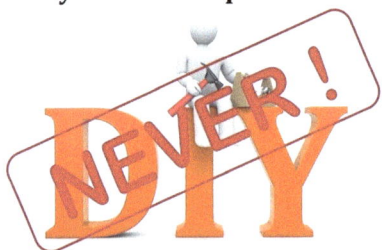

Many Years of Experience Rule 3: *Never* rely on the "I know a guy" option. Occasionally there are some very talented individuals out there who may be able to help you. But experience shows that such individuals usually move on. A few years later, you need support with his (or her) customisations – and he/she is nowhere to be found. This is a real business risk, often requiring a complete (and expensive) redo of much of the original work.

Many Years of Experience Rule 4: *Always* engage a competent, well recommended, consulting and implementation firm that specialises implementing such systems *in your industry sector*. (Just because a consulting firm has successfully implemented a certain technology in a number of financial institutions, does not imply that they understand the first thing about the business processes of a manufacturer, a professional practice or an oil refinery!)

An investment in genuine expertise will always deliver a good return on investment. Only when you are satisfied that you have chosen a reputable firm that understands the your business challenge and understands your industry, should you make your final choice of technology decision. And make that decision together with the chosen experts.

Of course I am not saying that the choice of which specific technology to select is unimportant. It must obviously offer all of the functionality that you require to solve your business problem. What I am saying is that an effective implementation, *assisted by real experts*, is ultimately far more important than chasing a specific brand of technology. This is the route to success.

6. Run an Alignment and Planning Workshop

Okay, the basics are now in place. We know what problem we are trying to solve and we have analysed the processes and the process changes necessary. We have chosen what we believe to be the ideal technology solution and we have chosen a proven, competent implementation partner. Now it's time to mobilise the people.

To stand any chance of success, we need everyone to be aligned – sharing and buying-in to the goals, strategy and plans. We need the relevant managers and employees to engage and become an active part of the process.

A very concerning outcome at this stage would be to have naysayers chirping on the side lines or – even worse – to have certain individuals attempting to sabotage the outcome, in the interests of pursuing their own personal agendas.

Experience has shown that the most effective way to promote alignment and buy-in is through an *inclusive* Alignment and Planning Workshop. Ensure however, that everyone even remotely concerned with the upcoming implementation is invited to attend. Exclusion very often leads to negativity, bitterness and possible attempts to derail the process. (Remember what happened to Sleeping Beauty!)

The agenda for the Alignment and Planning Workshop should be managed by a relevant and experienced external facilitator and should include at least:

- Introduction of the Problem Statement (in context of the organisation's Vision, Strategies and Goals).

- Introduction of the Business Process Analysis.

- Introduction of the Possible Enabling Technology Solutions.

- Workshop-style debate of the above, seeking consensus if possible.

- Introduction of the required elements of the Implementation Plan.

- Workshop-style formulation of the Implementation Plan.

- Buy-in and agreement from all to support and execute the project.

7. Formulate The Implementation Plan

The outcome of the Alignment and Planning Workshop should be majority acceptance of an agreed Implementation Plan. This Implementation Plan should include all the ingredients of a typical action/execution/project plan. In other words, it must clearly outline:

- What must be done

- By Whom

- By When.

The Plan should also clearly set out the critical success factors for the implementation and the key measurements and key performance indicators (KPIs) that will be used to determine success or failure of each project phase.

To fully succeed, the Implementation Plan must fully address the three essential business components, namely…

- **People**: The skills development and organisation structure changes necessary to effectively integrate the new technology into the business.

- **Processes**: The development of, or changes to, existing business and technical processes and methodologies to encourage adoption of, and make effective use of, the enabling technology.

- **Technology**: The procurement, installation, configuration and customisation of the enabling technology itself.

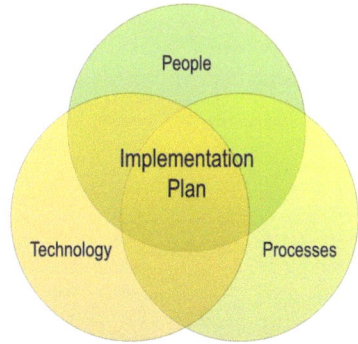

8. Execute The Implementation Plan

Just execute the plan! Sounds simple doesn't it? Of course, as you (and most other people in business) already know, execution is actually the most difficult step of all.

The main obstacles are going to be the natural resistance to change and people simply not doing what they are expected to do (for whatever reasons). The obstacles of resistance to change and failure to execute are so pervasive and so challenging, that the following chapter is devoted to the issues of how to overcome them.

9. Ensure Adoption

Assuming a successful implementation, this is the most important step in the process: Ensuring that the technology is adopted by all and becomes a normal, integral part of everyday operations. This is so important to ultimate success, that the entire content of the following chapter is dedicated to this topic.

10. Realise the Promise and Success

Diligently execute each of these steps in the process and you *will* be able to realise and enjoy the promise of the enabling technology and the expected success.

11. Measure, Improve, Continue

It is critical to bear in mind that a system underpinned by enabling technology is not a perpetual-motion machine. Active Leadership is needed to inject energy into the system; unexpected things *will* happen; circumstances *will* change; and things *will* go wrong (as Alice discovered in Wonderland!).

Our technology implementation must therefore be measured, evaluated and improved over time. In other words, the implementation should not be viewed as linear and finite. It is in fact circular, and we need to continuously start the process again when the inevitable changes in circumstance or opportunity occur. But more of this in the final chapter.

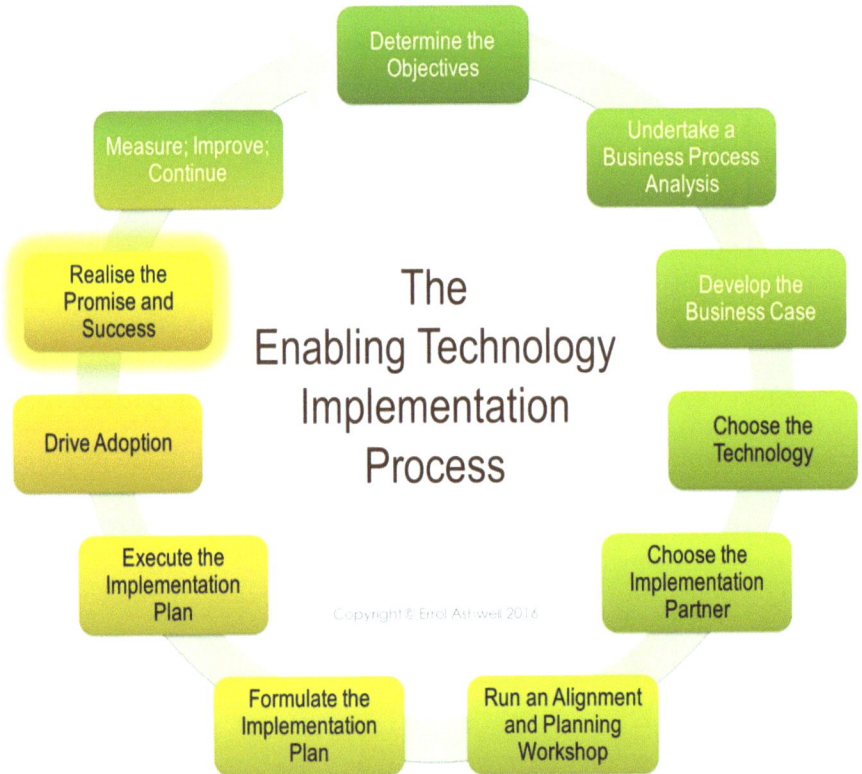

The
Enabling Technology
Implementation
Process

Determine the Objectives

Undertake a Business Process Analysis

Develop the Business Case

Choose the Technology

Choose the Implementation Partner

Run an Alignment and Planning Workshop

Formulate the Implementation Plan

Execute the Implementation Plan

Drive Adoption

Realise the Promise and Success

Measure; Improve; Continue

Copyright© Errol Ashwell 2016

10. Driving Execution

The Need For Execution

Very simply, execution is getting things done. It is a well-known adage that many organisations are "long on strategy, but short on execution". Another way of putting execution into perspective, is the no-nonsense adage "strategy plus execution equals success, while strategy without execution is pointless".

So too, of course, with implementing enabling technologies: During our discussion earlier about the Alignment and Planning Workshop, we highlighted that the key outcome should be the majority acceptance of an agreed Implementation Plan. However, *the plan is pointless unless it is executed*.

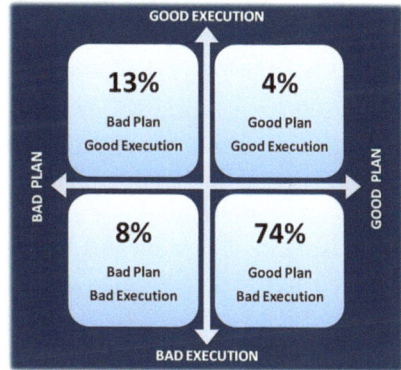

Typical Organisation Execution Experience
Dr Dick Ruhe – Blanchard LeaderChat Blog

As discussed previously, the Implementation Plan outlines What must be done; By Whom; By When. It also sets out the critical success factors for the implementation and the key performance indicators (KPIs) and measurements that will be used to determine success or failure for each phase. Now we need to ensure execution of the plan!

We need to create and develop a culture of execution: We need to ensure that every individual (By Whom) mentioned in the Implementation Plan diligently takes on their role and tasks (What) and executes them to the best of their ability on or before the expected deadlines (By When).

Simple, right? Well, yes – if they do execute correctly and on time. Unfortunately, the reality in most organisations is that daily life catches up, things are not done and deadlines are missed. This is what makes execution the most difficult step of all.

Creating a Culture of Execution

Ultimately, what every business needs is an overall culture of execution; not just great execution on a specific project or goal. Great execution needs to become an integral part of the organisation's culture, its DNA, in order to ensure success in every endeavour undertaken.

A culture of execution can be recognised when everyone in the team is constantly aware of goals and critical success factors; is able to prioritise and ensure that the critical activities are completed ahead of the everyday issues; and is ready to accept accountability for their actions – or lack thereof. This is the culture you need to create.

The 4 Disciplines of Execution

If you have not done so already, I would strongly recommend that you purchase yourself a copy of 'The 4 Disciplines of Execution' by Chris McChesney, Sean Covey and Jim Huling. This acclaimed book, based on years of practical consulting experience by the Franklin-Covey Organisation, is a must-read for anyone wishing to implement a culture of execution in any organisation.

The basic premise of their book is that while business strategy addresses the 'what' we need to do, it does not inform the 'how' we need to do it. The 'how' is the basis of execution – and in most businesses there will always be more good ideas than there is the capacity to execute them. Faced with the "Whirlwind" of everyday business requirements and activities, execution of new – even very important – initiatives and goals simply does not happen. Basically, the more you try to do, the less you actually accomplish.

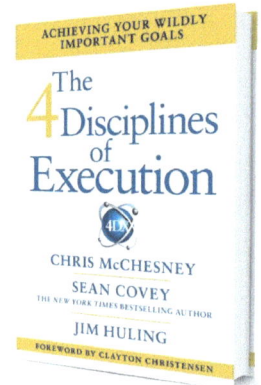

The authors have proven the need for four disciplines in any organisation to ensure execution of any key project, initiative or goal:

1. Focus on the 'Wildly Important' to keep the 'Whirlwind' at bay.

2. Act on 'Lead Measures' (rather than after-the-fact lag measures).

3. Ensure Engagement by keeping a 'Compelling Scoreboard'.

4. Create a 'Cadence of Accountability'.

To fully understand this methodology and put it into action, you need to read the book. It would not hurt to purchase copies for your entire management team (and get them to read it)!

The benefits of dramatically improved execution go way beyond implementing enabling technology. Your entire business will benefit dramatically. You will not regret it!

Executing the Implementation Plan

So back to our specific challenge – executing the Implementation Plan for our enabling technology project. Executing the Implementation Plan is a critical step in 'The Process'. It must succeed or we will never get to the next step – i.e. adopting the technology into our everyday operations in order to realise the promise and reap the rewards.

Scope, Deliverables and Outcomes

As we determined earlier, an outcome of the Alignment and Planning Workshop should be an agreed Implementation Plan. Such an Implementation Plan fully outlines the scope, deliverables and outcomes affecting each of the three essential business components, namely...

- **People**: The skills development and organisation structure changes necessary to effectively integrate the new technology into the business must be executed. Each individual must receive the appropriate training to ensure that they know how to use their aspect of the technology.

Expert assistance should be sought to come onsite and help workgroups, as a whole, understand how to make the technology work for the business; to show everyone the techniques, tips and tricks never taught during basic training; and to ensure that everyone uses the technology in a similar way to promote collaboration.

As an aside, any manager who says "I'm not going to pay to train them – they'll just leave and go work for my competition!" deserves the failure that he/she will undoubtedly receive.

The best quote that I have ever heard from a client on this topic is: "Question: What is worse than training your staff, then having them leave? Answer: *Not* training your staff and then having them stay!"

- **Processes**: The development of, or changes to, existing business and technical processes and methodologies to encourage adoption of and make effective use of the enabling technology must now be effectively executed and implemented.

- **Technology**: The procurement, installation, configuration and customisation of the enabling technology itself must be begun and executed as per the plan.

Leadership Role

We have discussed the meaning of Active Leadership and the key role that it plays in realising the promise of enabling technology. The role of Leadership remains critical during the execution of the Implementation Plan and includes...

- **The appointment of a Project Sponsor**: This is the member of the leadership who accepts accountability for the implementation of the project and the go-to person in the case of significant decisions to be made – such as requests for unforeseen expenditure or changes in project scope. Other leadership team members may well have to be involved in making such decisions.

- **The announcement and positioning of the project as a 'Wildly Important Goal (WIG)'**: It is the responsibility of the organisation leadership to inform the entire organisation of the project and to explain how important it is that it succeeds. Leadership must motivate and inspire everyone to contribute to the project's success in any way possible.

- **The appointment a Project Manager**: This is the key person, reporting to the Project Sponsor, who must manage (plan; organise; lead; control) the project team and ensure that the project is successfully delivered on time and within budget.

Project Manager Role

Depending upon the scope of the project, this role does not necessarily demand a professional full-time Project Manager. A smaller project can easily be handled part-time by an existing staff member. A knowledge of project management is certainly a requirement, but not necessarily a formal qualification.

For large projects a full-time Project Manager will be required. Such a person does not necessarily have to be a permanent employee. The person might well be an independent consultant.

With the overall goal of successfully delivering the project on time and within budget, the Project Manager role includes...

- **Plan; Organise; Lead; Control**: Documenting a formal project management plan. Deciding what must be done by whom and by when. Leading the project team and measuring actions and performance against the predetermined key performance indicators.

- **Escalating Decisions**: It is not within the role of the Project Manager to make non-operational or out-of-scope decisions. In such cases it is the Project Manager's responsibility to gather all the necessary information and present it to leadership in such a way that they are enabled to make an informed decision.

Cadence of Accountability

For any implementation project that is going to last longer than a week or two (and most do!) it is important to create that all-important 'cadence of accountability' as discussed earlier. Implementation projects have many moving parts and involve many people – both internal and external to the organisation. It is all too easy for people to get caught up in the daily 'Whirlwind' and let their project responsibilities slip.

A rhythm of regular meetings needs to be established (same time, same place) in order that project participants get used to being held accountable to their project colleagues for delivery of their part. Having to explain to all why their part of the process is ahead or behind is a powerful motivator to get people executing diligently and well.

EXECUTION OVER EXCUSES

11. Adoption Adoption Adoption

As mentioned before, only when there is widespread adoption of the technology can the system be deemed 'successful'. So is it possible to ensure adoption? The short answer is 'Yes'. Yes – if we never forget that adoption has virtually nothing to do with the technology and everything to do with people. As we all know, people need a good reason to embrace change. Looking at examples of successful technology implementations, one sees the presence of both 'carrot' and 'stick' elements to encourage adoption, backed by Active Leadership and a leadership-defined culture of use.

The Carrot

Prospective users of the system (at all levels) need to believe that they will personally benefit from using the technology (compared with whatever came before). The benefit need not necessarily be direct – e.g. using the new technology is quicker or easier than the old way. The benefit may well be an indirect reward – e.g. use the technology as intended to be recognised as a valued contributor towards the achievement of team goals.

The Stick

Organisation leadership needs to clearly communicate (and enforce) the message that full and proper use of the technology by everyone concerned is a requirement – and that there are consequences for non-compliance. This is a business imperative: *Most benefits of a new technology cannot be realised if use of the system is perceived to be 'optional'.*

Leadership-Defined Culture of Use

It is critical that the organisation leadership itself instils a culture of use of the technology. If it is perceived (rightly or wrongly) that the leadership never looks at relevant reports or dashboards, or does not care about the quality of the results, then the new solution ship is dead in the water. The technology needs to be used by everyone *and be seen to be used* by everyone.

The Challenge of Implementing Change

We all refer to our or other people's 'comfort zone'. As we know, this is a very real thing in life and especially in our work environment. There are things that we like to do and things that we do not. So it is quite natural in any workplace to find people settled into a comfortable routine – perhaps even complacent.

There is nothing that is going to challenge somebody's comfort and complacency more than adding change into their lives. Change disturbs the norm; change requires effort; and change is not normally viewed as a good thing. Change is seldom welcomed with open arms! Change is a constant in life and particularly in business. It's how we manage and deal with change that makes it good or bad.

Change is often specifically needed to meet a challenge or make an improvement. Now, when we decide to initiate a specific change, we also – automatically – inherit the necessity to lead and manage that change.

Even if you believe that the change is for the good and that the benefits of the change should be obvious to all, beware: Not everyone will agree with you and you will encounter resistance to the change.

The process of persuading people to embrace and adopt change takes both leadership and management, where leadership is the process of aligning, inspiring, motivating and mobilising.

Implementing new enabling technology is no exception. People will need to be inspired, motivated, persuaded and encouraged to adopt the new technology and the process changes required to makes its use a success. Once again, *Active Leadership* is the key to implementing change. The leader must be – and be seen to be – actively, meaningfully and enthusiastically involved at all times.

Making Change Happen.

Effectively leading change will require you to pay particular attention to the following leadership and management attributes:

- **Understanding**: Your current processes may have been in place for a long time. People need to understand why the change is necessary and how they and the organisation will benefit. Be sensitive to reactions and explore what is behind resistance or concerns.

- **Courage**: Change will bring risks and fears. A big part of being a successful agent of change is helping people to put such risks and fears into perspective. Don't deny their existence, simply help the individuals to see them in a different light. Help them to be courageous in the face of change. Help them to see a glass half full, not half empty.

- **Flexibility**: In a situation of major change, nobody can foresee every situation. Problems and challenges will arise that nobody considered. It is possible that the plan or process may have to be slightly changed. Demonstrate flexibility and agility in responding to such situations. That does not mean capitulating and giving up on the entire plan, it simply means being prepared to tweak when tweaking is necessary.

- **Recognition**: There is probably no better way to motivate change than recognition. Recognise those who are making the change and making the difference. It does not matter whether it is a quiet word or a public gesture, recognising those who are successfully adopting the change will gradually inspire others to follow suit.

Successful adoption of an enabling technology ultimately requires everyone to embrace the change.

Global Change Leadership Best Practice.

This book is certainly not meant to fully cover the vast subject of 'change'. My goal is simply to highlight the importance of change leadership and management when considering and implementing a new enabling technology.

In fact, I would strongly recommend that if you have not done so already, purchase yourself a copy of 'Our Iceberg is Melting' by Dr. John Kotter and Holger Rathgeber. This iconic book is a must-read for anyone facing the challenges of change in an organisation and outlines the methodology and processes to make change really happen.

With every credit to the authors, I quote here the eight key steps that Kotter and Rathgeber explain are needed to get the people in your organisation to accept and implement change. This is fundamental to ensuring the effective adoption of any new enabling technology and attendant processes.

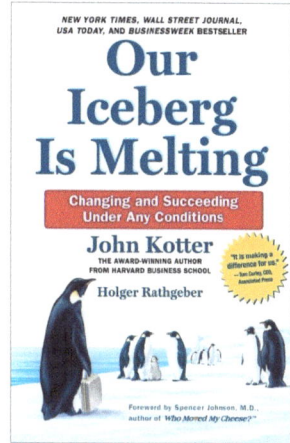

Kotter's Eight Step Process of Successful Change

1. Create a Sense of Urgency
2. Develop the Guiding Team
3. Develop a Change Vision & Strategy
4. Communicate the Vision Buy-in
5. Empower Broad-based Action
6. Produce Short-term Wins
7. Don't Let Up
8. Make Change Stick

It is important to note that this summary does not tell you enough – or explain how to put this methodology properly into action. You need to purchase and read the book. It is an easy, quick read – and you will not regret it!

12. Realising the Promise

Once everyone begins to appreciate the benefits of the new system, widespread adoption *will* begin. Marketers will see improved results; salespeople will see bigger commission pay-outs and leaders will enjoy meaningful information to keep their fingers on the pulse of the business. The organisation is poised to realise the full promise of the enabling technology implementation.

As we know, the return on an investment in enabling technology will only be realised if and when the business outcomes – as set out in the business case – are realised. When the requisite changes in behaviour and business outcomes begin to happen, then you will have an implementation that 'works'. However, these business outcomes will only be realised when Active Leadership paves the way and *demands that the results should be realised.*

When widespread adoption of the technology is realised throughout your business, the solution will be 'successful'. You will have achieved something that many organisations fail to achieve. You will have realised the promise of enabling technology – a 'giant leap in performance and capability'. Any you will have enabled your organisation to enjoy a significant competitive advantage! Enjoy and celebrate your success!

13. Live Long and Prosper

So what is next? Keep in mind that it is better (*much* better) to end up with a simple system that works and is adopted, than to embark on the implementation of a complex system that never comes to fruition. In his book 'Systemantics: How Systems Really Work and How They Fail' John Gall states: "A complex system that works is invariably found to have evolved from a simple system that worked. A complex system designed from scratch never works and cannot be patched up to make it work. You have to start over with a working simple system." This has now become known as Gall's Law.

This law explains the success of systems like the World Wide Web and Blogosphere, which grew from simple to complex (and widely adopted) systems incrementally and, in some ways, organically. This is a powerful lesson for us. The road to successfully underpinning your business with enabling technology is to do so carefully and incrementally. Once a system is successfully adopted, only then should you move on to the next implementation.

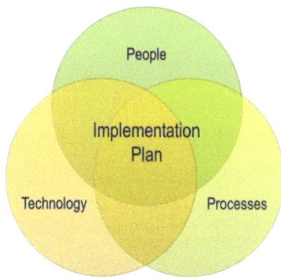

We have examined that technology alone is seldom (if ever) the answer. Considering together the aspects of people, processes and technology builds resilience into your business and prepares it to take advantage of opportunities that present themselves.

We have also examined that a system underpinned by enabling technology is not a perpetual-motion machine. Even though our new system is working, adopted and successful, Active Leadership is still needed to inject energy into the system. Active Leadership is also needed to deal with the real-world realities: Unexpected things will happen; circumstances will change; and anything that can go wrong, will.

All systems change, and complex systems are constantly in a state of flux. Change is a fact of life. We cannot usually plan for specific change as many changes arrive unexpectedly. However, we should learn to expect change and plan to cope with change when it does arrive.

So what am I really saying here? I am suggesting that implementing enabling technologies is a journey, not a destination. Just when you think that you are finished, there is always the next phase; the next opportunity; the next new technology innovation; or the need to cope with the next unexpected circumstance or external business challenge.

Two of these challenges are typically out of your direct control – but demand Active Leadership reaction:

- Changes in the external business environment may change completely the way you need to work and the technology needed to support that way of working. You may need technology changes to enable new competitive advantage or to retain the competitive advantage that you have already gained.

- The invention and availability of new 'disruptive' technologies can also wipe out your current competitive advantage – or offer the opportunity to gain new advantage.

Consider companies involved in the oil or mining industry. These businesses are constantly having to react as the price of oil or mineral commodities goes up and down. Of course there are also numerous interdependencies with other industries, so those environmental changes often ripple throughout the economy. The judicious use of enabling technologies can maximise the ability of companies to react effectively to such environmental changes.

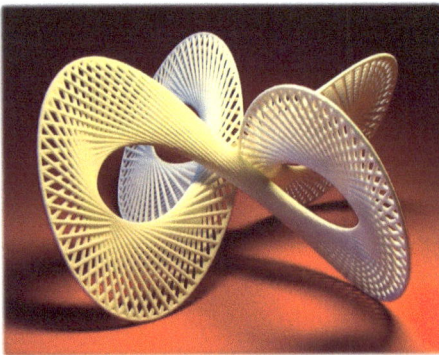

10-YEAR CRUDE OIL PRICES
U.S. DOLLARS PER BARREL (WTI)

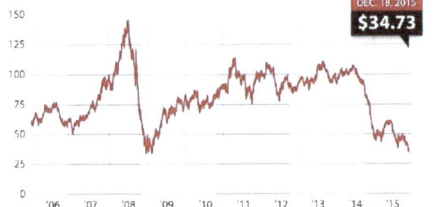

DEC. 18, 2015
$34.73

An example of a disruptive technology now offering many new opportunities is 'additive manufacturing' (also commonly known as '3D printing'). This technology has completely changed the way that many products can be made and has opened up significant new avenues of opportunity from space vehicles to the medical and scientific fields – and has become an enabler for the new small manufacturer 'maker movement'. An opportunity for competitive advantage? Certainly huge for some!

So realising the promise of enabling technology is an on-going process. We need to plan for and enjoy successive, perhaps smaller wins. Aim for the big prize by executing and succeeding with incremental steps. Value agility and be prepared to constantly measure, evaluate, improve and course-correct when necessary. But always follow 'The Process'.

May you live long and prosper – and *enable your competitive advantage* by realising the promise of enabling technology!

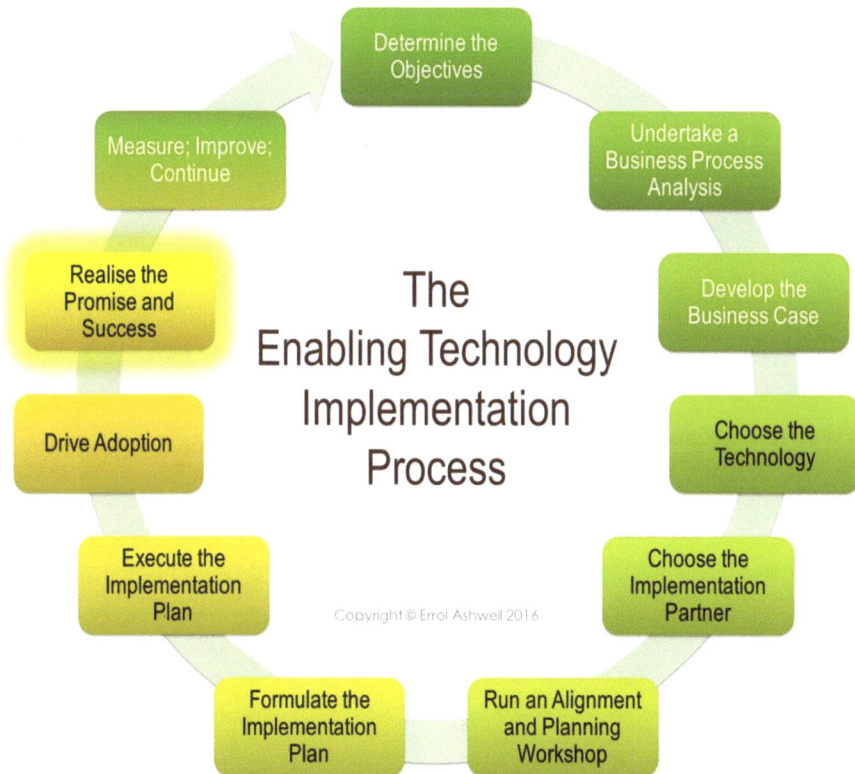

The Enabling Technology Implementation Process

- Determine the Objectives
- Undertake a Business Process Analysis
- Develop the Business Case
- Choose the Technology
- Choose the Implementation Partner
- Run an Alignment and Planning Workshop
- Formulate the Implementation Plan
- Execute the Implementation Plan
- Drive Adoption
- Realise the Promise and Success
- Measure; Improve; Continue

Copyright © Errol Ashwell 2016

14. Personal Support and Consultation

I trust that you found the contents of this book useful and that it helps you on your journey towards success and significant competitive advantage!

Do not hesitate to contact me should you need professional assistance with any of the activities and processes described in this book:

- Consulting.
- Problem analysis.
- Interviews and focus group facilitation.
- Business process analysis.
- Technology selection.
- Implementation planning.
- Board presentations.
- Staff presentations.
- Function presentations.
- Workshop preparation and facilitation.
- Project participation.

Give me a call or drop me an email...

- Telephone: +27 82 888 0636
- Email: errol@ashwell.co.za

Errol Ashwell

Shelly Beach, KwaZulu-Natal, South Africa. 2016.

Illustration, Image and Photograph Credits / Attribution

Page	Image	Credit / Attribution
5	1	By Andrew Bell, courtesy Paragon Architects
9	1	By Newton Henry Black, Harvey Nathaniel Davis [Public domain], via Wikimedia Commons
10	1	By Eye Steel Film from Canada [CC BY 2.0 (http://creativecommons.org/licenses/by/2.0)], via Wikimedia Commons
11	1	By Farm Security Administration [Public domain], via Wikimedia Commons
12	1	Courtesy Salesforce.com® Marketing
13	1	Courtesy Adept Airmotive®
14	1	By Own Oil Industry News [Public domain], via Wikimedia Commons
15	1	By CarpathianPrince [Royalty Free], via BigStockImages.com
15	2	By Errol Ashwell © All Rights Reserved
16	1	By Errol Ashwell © All Rights Reserved
16	2	By Dometorres [CC BY-SA 4.0 (http://creativecommons.org/licenses/by/4.0)], via Wikimedia Commons
17	1	By Steve Jurvetson [CC BY 2.0 (http://creativecommons.org/licenses/by/2.0)], via Flickr.com
18	1	Courtesy Autodesk® Marketing
19	1	[Public domain], via BusinessImagesFree.com
20	1	By violetkaipa [Royalty Free], via BigStockImages.com
21	1	By Jurgen Appelo [CC BY 2.0 (http://creativecommons.org/licenses/by/2.0)], via Flickr.com
22	1	By Ambrophoto [Royalty Free], via BigStockImages.com
23	1	By iqoncept [Royalty Free], via BigStockImages.com
24	1	By hildgrim [CC BY 2.0 (http://creativecommons.org/licenses/by/2.0)], via Flickr.com
25	1	By digitalista [Royalty Free], via BigStockImages.com
26	1	By Dave Jefferys [CC BY 2.0 (http://creativecommons.org/licenses/by/2.0)], via Flickr.com
27	1	By Ted [CC BY 2.0 (http://creativecommons.org/licenses/by/2.0)], via Flickr.com
28	1	By Tom Davie [CC BY-SA 4.0 (http://creativecommons.org/licenses/by/4.0)], via Béhance.net
28	2	By PlusONE [Royalty Free], via BigStockImages.com
29	1	By Yuri [Royalty Free], via BigStockImages.com
31	1	By Arcady31 [Royalty Free], via BigStockImages.com
32	1	By Palto [Royalty Free], via BigStockImages.com
32	2	By Jacob Wackerhausen [Royalty Free], via BigStockImages.com
33	1	By Mace Ojala [CC BY 2.0 (http://creativecommons.org/licenses/by/2.0)], via Flickr.com
33	2	By docstockmedia [Royalty Free], via ShutterStock.com
35	1	By Errol Ashwell © All Rights Reserved
36	1	By Errol Ashwell © All Rights Reserved
37	1	Courtesy Dr Dick Ruhe, Blanchard Leaderchat Blog
38	1	By Matt Ryall [CC BY 2.0 (http://creativecommons.org/licenses/by/2.0)], via Flickr.com
38	2	Courtesy FranklinCovey® Marketing
39	1	By Goodluz [Royalty Free], via BigStockImages.com
40	1	[Public domain]
41	1	By Wavebreak Media Ltd [Royalty Free], via BigStockImages.com
42	1	[Public domain]
43	1	By Chuck Grimmett [CC BY 2.0 (http://creativecommons.org/licenses/by/2.0)], via Flickr.com
43	2	By Daxiao Productions [Royalty Free], via BigStockImages.com
45	1	Courtesy Kotter International® Marketing
45	2	By stockphoto-graf [Royalty Free], via ShutterStock.com
46	1	By Rawpixel.com [Royalty Free], via BigStockImages.com
47	1	By Errol Ashwell © All Rights Reserved
48	1	Courtesy The Canadian Press
48	2	By fdecomite [CC BY 2.0 (http://creativecommons.org/licenses/by/2.0)], via Flickr.com
49	1	By Errol Ashwell © All Rights Reserved
51	1	[Public domain]

Notes